David Beckham

Blue
Band

Please return
on or before
the last date
stamped below

Published in association with The Basic Skills Agency

Hodder & Stoughton

A MEMBER OF THE HODDER HEADLINE GROUP

Acknowledgements

Cover: All Action

Photos: pp 2, 6, 10, 13, 26 Allstar; p 17 Matthew Ashton/Empics Ltd;
p 20 Tony Marshall/Empics Ltd; p 23 Popperfoto/Reuters

Every effort has been made to trace copyright holders of material reproduced in this book. Any
rights not acknowledged will be acknowledged in subsequent printings if notice is given to the
publisher.

Orders: please contact Bookpoint Ltd, 130 Milton Park, Abingdon, Oxon OX14 4SB. Telephone:
(44) 01235 400414, Fax: (44) 01235 400454. Lines are open from 9.00–6.00, Monday to
Saturday, with a 24 hour message answering service.
Email address: orders@bookpoint.co.uk

British Library Cataloguing in Publication Data
A catalogue record for this title is available from the British Library

ISBN 0 340 77623 4

First published 2000
Impression number   10 9 8 7 6 5 4 3 2
Year   2005 2004 2003 2002 2001

Copyright © 2000 Andy Croft

Typeset by GreenGate Publishing Services, Tonbridge, Kent.
Printed in Great Britain for Hodder and Stoughton Educational, a division of Hodder Headline
Plc, 338 Euston Road, London NW1 3BH, by **The Bath Press, Bath**

Contents

1 Childhood

David Robert Joseph Beckham was born
in London on 2 May 1975.
He grew up in Leytonstone,
in the East End.

He went to Chase Lane Juniors
and Chingford High School.
David Beckham was never very good at school-work.
He just wanted to be a footballer.

David Beckham

The nearest big clubs to David Beckham
were Spurs and West Ham.
But David Beckham's dad
supported Manchester United.
So did David Beckham.
He wanted to play for Manchester United.
He wanted to play at Old Trafford.
He was crazy about Manchester United.
David Beckham's hero was Manchester United
captain Bryan Robson.
He used to watch Manchester United when they
played in London.
When Manchester United played at West Ham,
David Beckham was
the Manchester United mascot!

When David Beckham was eight he played for
Ridgeway Rovers.
They were good. They once won 23–0!
He also played for Waltham Forest and
for Essex schoolboys.
The local paper called him
the 'Chingford football sensation'.

When David Beckham was eleven
he entered a competition.
It was run by Bobby Charlton's Coaching School.
Kids from all over the country took part.
To win you needed good ball control.
David Beckham reached the final.
Guess where it was? Old Trafford!

Bobby Charlton was amazed.
David Beckham was the best eleven-year-old
he had ever seen.
David Beckham won the competition.
The prize was a two week holiday in Spain,
at the Nou Camp stadium in Barcelona.
There he met Gary Lineker,
Mark Hughes and Terry Venables.

Bobby Charlton

2 Signing On

London clubs soon heard about the boy wonder.
He had trials with Spurs and Leyton Orient.
Spurs wanted to sign him.
But David Beckham only wanted to play
for Manchester United.

One day he was playing for Waltham Forest.
A scout from Manchester United saw the game.
United asked him for a trial.
They liked what they saw.
On 2 May 1991 Alex Ferguson
signed him for United.
It was David Beckham's sixteenth birthday.

3 Old Trafford

The Reds had some very famous players:
Bryan Robson,
Mark Hughes,
Dennis Irwin,
Steve Bruce,
Brian McClair,
Gary Pallister,
Paul Ince,
Lee Sharpe,
Andrei Kanchelskis and
Ryan Giggs.

United had just won the Cup-Winners' Cup.
Alex Ferguson wanted to win the Championship.
He was planning for the future.
He had some brilliant young players.
They spent all their time practising.

No-one had heard of them in those days.
They have now:
    Paul Scholes,
    Gary Neville,
    Phil Neville,
    Nicky Butt,
    Robbie Savage,
    Keith Gillespie and
    David Beckham.

In 1992 United's Youth team won the FA Youth Cup.
David Beckham scored in the final.

David Beckham still amazes people with his skills.

4 First Team Football

In October 1992 David Beckham played
in the first team.
He came on as a substitute against Brighton
in the League Cup.
He was just seventeen.

The next season
he did not play for the first team at all –
just for the Reserves.
That season Manchester United
won the Reserves' League.

Alex Ferguson wanted to give
his young players first-team football.
David Beckham went on loan to Preston North End.
He played only four games for Preston
but he scored twice.
He was Man of the Match three times.

David Beckham didn't play a full game for United
until April 1995.
It was against Leeds,
at Old Trafford.

5 Number 7

David Beckham was soon a regular in the first team.
He played right midfield and
scored eight goals in his first full season.
He scored against Chelsea
in the FA Cup semi-final.
In the Cup Final
Cantona scored the winning goal
from a Beckham cross.
That season Manchester United won the Double.

The next season United were Champions again.
David Beckham scored twelve goals.
He scored his most famous goal
against Wimbledon.
The Wimbledon keeper was off his line.
David Beckham tried a shot from the half-way line.
It went in!

Celebrating David Beckham's famous goal against Wimbledon.

He scored another amazing goal against Chelsea.
He hit the ball so hard
it went in at about 99 miles per hour.
David Beckham was voted Young Player of the Year.

At the end of the season Eric Cantona retired.
Who was going to wear his Number 7 shirt?
David Beckham.
Just like his hero Bryan Robson,
he wore it for the Charity Shield match.
By mistake, his name was spelt BECKAM
on the shirt!
That season he scored eleven goals
and he only missed one league game.

6 Europe

Alex Ferguson had won everything
except the Champions' League.

Manchester United reached the quarter-finals.
They reached the semi-finals –
but they could not get any further.
In 1997 they reached the semi-finals again
but were knocked out.

In 1998–1999 it was different.
Manchester United beat LKS Lodz.
They put eleven goals past Brondby.
David Beckham scored.
They drew with Barcelona.
David Beckham scored.
They drew with Bayern Munich.

United beat Inter Milan in the quarter-final.
Dwight Yorke scored twice from Beckham's crosses.

They beat Juventus in the semi-final.
Roy Keane scored from a Beckham corner.

They met Bayern Munich again in the final.
The game was at the Nou Camp in Barcelona.
About 90,000 people saw the game live.
Millions watched it on TV.

Bayern Munich were winning 1–0.
The game went into injury time.
Then Teddy Sherringham equalised.
Bayern Munich could not believe it.
Two minutes later Manchester United scored again.

Man United were European Champions!

Manchester United win the European Championship in 1999.

7 England

In 1996 England had a new manager.
His name was Glen Hoddle.
Hoddle wanted David Beckham to play for England.
David Beckham played in all the qualifying matches.
Once he was booked
for not getting onto a stretcher.

In 1998 David Beckham was picked to go to France
for the World Cup.

He played as a wing-back against Tunisia.
England won 2–0.
He played in midfield against Colombia.
David Beckham took a free kick.
He curled the ball around the wall.
It beat the Colombian keeper.
It was a fantastic goal! England won 2–0.
David Beckham was a national hero!

In the next round England played Argentina.
After only six minutes
Argentina were given a penalty.
Batistuta scored.
A few minutes later
England were given a penalty.
Alan Shearer scored.
Then Michael Owen scored for England.
It looked like England
were going to win the game.
Then disaster struck.

Diego Simeone tackled David Beckham.
It was a bad tackle.
David Beckham went down.
David Beckham kicked Simeone.
The referee saw it.
He brought out a red card.
David Beckham was sent off.

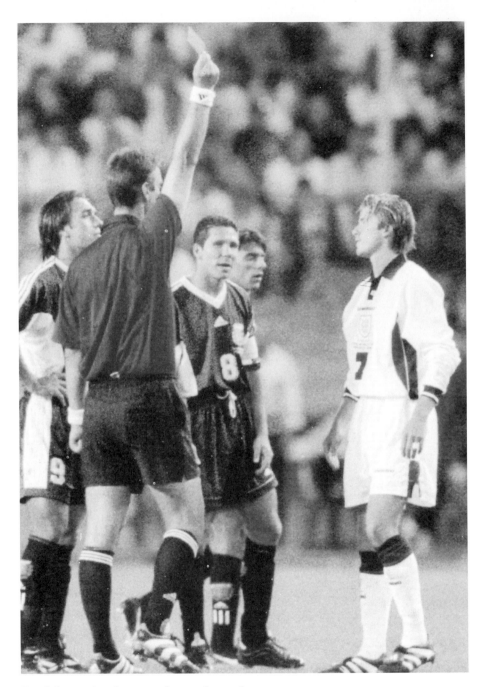

Beckham is shown the red card.

He had never been sent off before.
Argentina soon scored again.
England were knocked out on penalties.

All the English fans were very upset.
Some fans were angry.
Some fans blamed David Beckham.

They forgot his brilliant goal
against Colombia.

8 Fame

It's hard being famous.

In 1997 David Beckham met Victoria Adams.
She is one of the Spice Girls –
better known as Posh Spice.
He saw her on a Spice Girl video.
Guess where they first met?
That's right. Old Trafford!

It was love at first sight.
They tried to keep it secret.
But the press soon found out.
Newspaper and television reporters
followed them everywhere.
They still do.

Beckham and Posh Spice at a show during London
fashion week.

He bought her a cross worth £25,000.
They bought a house worth £400,000.

In March 1999 Victoria gave birth
to a baby boy.
They called him Brooklyn.

In July 1999 Victoria and David were married.
The wedding was held in a castle in Ireland.
There was a firework display, and
an orchestra playing Spice Girl hits.
The Spice Girls were there.
All the Manchester United players were there.
Gary Neville was the best man.
Even the priest wore Manchester United socks!

9 Fortune

David Beckham plays for
the biggest football club in the world.
He plays for his country and
scores amazing goals.
He is the best crosser in the game and
the highest-paid footballer in Britain.

His goal against Spurs brought the title
back to Manchester United in 1999.
It was their fifth title in seven years.
That season they won the Treble.
They won the Championship, the FA Cup
and the European Champions' League.

David Beckham is a success.

David Beckham drives a Porsche.
He models clothes.
He is married to a pop-star.
His favourite food is sticky toffee pudding
and butterscotch sauce.

He is handsome, talented,
famous, lucky, successful
and very, very rich.
What's more, he's still only in his twenties.

Some people think he is a hero.
Some people don't like him.
Some people envy him.

But everyone agrees,
David Beckham is a brilliant footballer.

Key Dates

2 May 1975	David Beckham born
1986	Wins football competition and holiday to Nou Camp stadium in Barcelona
2 May 1991	Signed up to play for Manchester United
1992	Scores in FA Youth Cup Final
October 1992	Plays in the first team against Brighton
April 1995	Plays first full game for Manchester United
1996	Helps Manchester United win the Double
1997	Voted Young Player of the Year
1998	Gets sent off against Argentina in the World Cup 1998
1999	Manchester United wins the Treble
March 1999	His son, Brooklyn, born
July 1999	Marries Victoria Adams ('Posh Spice')